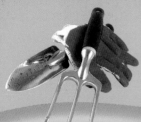

Grow *your own*

Tomatoes

Helen Lanz

LLYFRGELL ... REF SIROL WRECSAM
WREXHAM COUNTY BOROUGH LIBRARY SERVICE

TYNNWYD
O'R STOC

WITHDRAWN
FROM STOCK

W

FRANKLIN WAT

LONDON•SYDNEY

D1349455

First published in 2010
by Franklin Watts

Copyright © Franklin Watts 2010

Franklin Watts
338 Euston Road
London NW1 3BH

Franklin Watts Australia
Level 17/207 Kent Street
Sydney, NSW 2000

To Carolyn — thank goodness your support
is more reliable than my tomato canes

All rights reserved.

Series editor: Sarah Peutrill
Art director: Jonathan Hair
Design: Jane Hawkins
Photography: Victoria Coombs/Ecoscene (unless otherwise credited)

Credits: Brian J Abela/Shutterstock: f cover b. Chrislofoto/Shutterstock: f cover t.
Makai Dunne/istockphoto: 23b. Leon Forado/Shutterstock: 7cr. Roman Ivaschenko/
istockphoto: 27cr. Helen Lanz: endpapers (2, 31), 13t, 25tl, 25tr. Lisa McCorkle/istockphoto:
6t. Penny Oakley: endpapers (1, 32), 22b, 25b. Francesco Ridolfi/istockphoto: f cover b/g.
Ariel Skelley/Corbis: 3. Alexey Sokolov/istockphoto: 27b. Friedrich Stauss/Alamy: 18t. David
Taylor/Alamy: 24b. Sophia Tsibikaki/istockphoto: 26b. Rob Walls/Alamy: 23c.

Every attempt has been made to clear copyright. Should there be any inadvertent
omission please apply to the publisher for rectification.

The author and publisher would like to thank the models who took part in this book.

Thanks to Jasmine Clarke and Tony Field, seasoned gardeners, for kindly sharing their
gardening knowledge.

Dewey number: 635.6'42
ISBN: 978 0 7496 9296 4

Printed in China

Franklin Watts is a division of Hachette Children's Books, an Hachette UK company.
www.hachette.co.uk

WREXHAM C.B.C LIBRARY	
LLYFRGELL B.S. WRECSAM	
C56 0000 0496 145	
ASKEWS & HOLT	12-May-2011
J635.642	£12.99
JNF	WR

Safety notice:

Gardening is fun! There are a few basic rules you should always follow, however. Always garden with an adult; any pesticides and fertilisers should be handled by adults only and applied to specified plants only; wear appropriate clothing and footwear and always wash your hands when you have finished in the garden.

Contents

Words in **bold** are in the glossary on page 29.

Why grow your own tomatoes?

Do you like to eat salads in the summer? What are your favourite salad ingredients? Sweet peppers, lettuce or perhaps tomatoes?

▲ Most tomatoes are juicy and delicious in a sandwich or salad.

▲ Not all tomatoes are red; you can get yellow, orange, white and even browny-coloured ones.

Size and colour

Did you know that there are thousands of **varieties** of tomato? They vary in size from enormous beef tomatoes to tiny cherry tomatoes, and in colour from yellow to red. Flavours vary too. The small cherry tomatoes can be sweet tasting; some of the bigger varieties have a 'fruity' taste.

Grow your own

Have you ever thought about growing tomatoes? It really is a great journey to go on, one of flavour, colour, shape and size, and smell, too.

▲ When you water a tomato plant, it gives off an amazing smell.

◀ ▼ These are the main parts of a tomato plant.

Truss

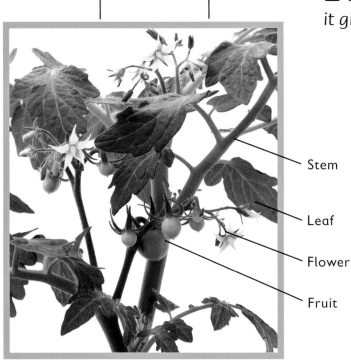

Stem

Leaf

Flower

Fruit

Root

Root hair

Fruit or vegetable?

A tomato is actually a fruit, not a vegetable, because it has **seeds** (see page 10). However, we think of it as a vegetable and eat it with salad.

Seed

Be prepared!

You've decided to go for it. Growing your own is great fun. You will get plenty of fresh air and have the pleasure of watching something that you've grown from seed grow into something that you can actually eat.

Thinking ahead

It's worth thinking about what you will need. For yourself, you will need some old clothes that your parents or carers won't mind if you get dirty, including some wellies or old trainers.

▲ You could wear gloves, but you don't have to.

▼ You will *need* plant pots to sow your seeds in.

You can grow tomatoes in containers, **grow-bags** or a vegetable plot. If you choose containers you will need some **compost** and **fertiliser**.

▶ If you are growing in containers, you will need to feed your tomatoes with a liquid fertiliser.

▲ Try to get a grow-bag that is thick, with plenty of soil in it.

▶ You will *definitely* need some tomato seeds!

◀ Some types of tomatoes need support from canes as they grow.

Top tip!

It's a good idea to keep a growing diary, writing down everything from the tomato variety to how and when you did things. This will help if you decide to do it again, and will be fun to look back on. If you have a camera, you could take pictures as well.

All about the seed

▲ You can expect to be picking your tomato harvest about 20 weeks after sowing your seeds.

There are so many different varieties of tomato, it can be difficult to know which one to grow. Use the Internet or ask at your local garden centre for advice.

Tall or bush type?

There are indoor and outdoor tomato plants and two main types – cordon (tall) or bush plants. Cordon plants grow well in the ground or grow-bags, needing a cane, or tall stick, to help them keep upright. Bush tomatoes grow better in pots, or hanging baskets off the ground because their fruit dangles down. As a beginner, it might be best to go for a variety that is **hardy**, or quite tough.

SCIENCE SPOT

Seeds

Seeds are embryo, or baby, plants: inside the tiny seed case is all the information needed to grow into the adult plant. A seed waits until the **conditions** are right for it to **germinate**, or start to grow. It usually needs to be dark, damp and warm.

Step-by-step

1. You will need to start your tomato seeds off inside.

2. Prepare your pots. If they aren't new, wash them out so they don't pass on any **diseases** to your young tomato plants. Almost fill to the top with compost. Make sure your compost is fine so your tomato seeds don't have to struggle to grow around large lumps of soil. You can 'sieve' the compost through the holes in a plant pot to remove lumps.

3. Water and leave overnight – this allows the soil to settle and makes sure it is moist (slightly damp) for the seeds.

4. Space four or five seeds evenly in the pot. Lightly cover with compost.

5. Cover your pot with cling film and place on a windowsill somewhere warm and sunny.

Encouraging growth

▲ It's fine to lift the cling film to see if your seeds have started to grow.

Check your seeds every day – it's important to keep the soil moist at all times. Be sure to water the seeds evenly and don't let the soil get too wet, or waterlogged.

Shoots

After about eight days, you should see little **shoots**. It's so exciting when you see a little green shoot appear.

SCIENCE SPOT *Germination*

Germination is the point when a seed starts to grow, breaking out of its seed case. The seed stays dormant, or asleep, until the conditions are right for it to grow. When the seed germinates, usually the root is the first thing to break through the seed case. The cotyledon, or seed leaf, also begins to grow, often becoming the first green leaves of the plant.

▲ Be patient! It may take some seeds a while to germinate.

Lots of light

As the shoots start to grow, remove the cling film. Make sure your **seedlings** are getting as much light as possible.

▶ *A windowsill is a good place to put your seedlings.*

◀ *The seedlings will grow towards the light. You might want to turn the plant pot occasionally.*

Top tip!

If the seed 'coat', or husk, sticks to the leaf, stopping it from opening properly, put a drop of water on the husk to soften it. This might help the leaf to push it off as it grows. Try not to pull it off as this might damage the leaf.

Pricking out

▲ *This seedling has two proper leaves, with two more leaves forming.*

About two weeks after sowing, your seedlings will probably want a bit more room to grow. When they have grown at least two proper leaves, move them to a (10cm) pot of their own. This is called pricking out.

Top tip!

When the seedlings start to grow, choose only the healthy, strong ones to **plant on**. This means you have the best chance of growing healthy plants.

Step-by-step

1. Fill each new pot with compost and water it, as you did before. Poke your finger, or the end of a pencil, into the soil in the middle of the pot.

2. Gently grasp one seedling by its leaves (not the stem as it might break), and lift it from its original pot. Or you could use an old spoon to scoop up a seedling, including some of the soil underneath it.

3. Place the seedling into the hole you have just made and gently, but firmly, push the soil around the stem.

4. Repeat this with your other seedlings. As they grow, space them out along the windowsill so their leaves don't touch. It's useful to mark each pot with the variety of tomato if you are growing different ones.

Preparing to plant out

▲ The clusters of flowers are called 'trusses'.

About a month after pricking out, when your plants are 15–25cm tall, or clusters of flowers begin to grow, they are ready to be planted into your vegetable plot or grow-bags.

Hardening off

It is a good idea to put the pots outside on sunny days, bringing them in at night, to get them used to being outside. This is called hardening off.

Find the right spot

Tomato plants like sunny, **sheltered** spots, so make sure your grow-bag or pot is put in the right place. It is best to do this before you plant out your tomatoes.

▲ Make sure there are no more frosty nights before the plants are placed outside all the time.

Step-by-step

Preparing a grow-bag:

1. Be sure to give the grow-bag a good shake to loosen the compost.

2. Ask a grown up to cut away three square holes – there are usually marks on the bag that act as a guide.

3. Make three small holes in the soil with your trowel or hand, ready for the plants.

Preparing a pot:

4. You can use a (25cm) pot or hanging basket. Fill these with soil (you will need a liner for the basket) and make one hole in the middle.

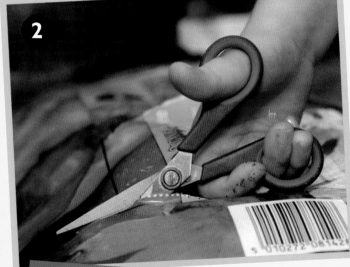

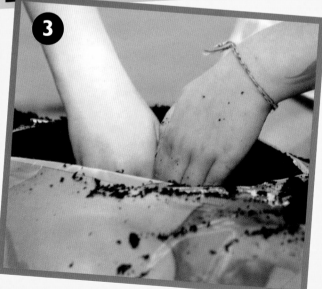

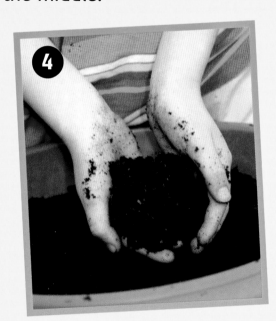

Planting out

Your young tomato plants are ready to plant out now.

Top tip!
The fruit from bush tomato plants may trail on the ground. To help keep them free from disease, plant them higher up in pots or hanging baskets.

▲ *These bush tomatoes tumble down the sides of the hanging basket as they grow.*

Step-by-step

1. Take one of your plants. Gently take hold of it by the stem and pull it out of its pot, being careful not to damage its roots.

2. Place the plant into the hole you made earlier, in your grow-bag or pot. Gently but firmly press the soil around the plant.

3. Plant a second and third tomato plant in this way in a grow-bag. You will need to leave about 40cm of space between each plant, so they can grow properly.

4. With a sharp pencil, poke holes along both ends of the grow-bag, and in between the plants. This allows water to drain out, so the soil does not get too soggy.

5. Give your tomato plants a drink!

Top tip!

If you only want two plants, you could use the central space of the grow-bag to sink an empty plant pot. Keep this topped up with water to keep the soil moist for the two plants at either end of the grow-bag.

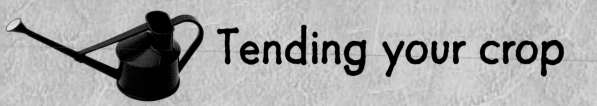

Be sure to check your tomato plants every day – the healthier they are, the better the harvest.

▶ *If the soil is dry on top but still soggy underneath, do not water yet.*

When to water

Check to see if your plants need watering by pushing your fingers into the soil. If the soil is dry, you need to water the plants.

When you are watering, check your plant over and remove any dead leaves. Look out for problems (see pages 22–23).

▶ *When you water your tomato plants, you're sure to notice the strong scent they give off.*

Give support

Cordon varieties need a cane to help them grow upright. Push the cane into the soil close to the plant. To help you see the top of the cane when you are watering, stick some brightly-coloured masking tape to the top. Be careful not to poke your eyes!

Gently attach a tie to the stem of the plant and the cane in one or two places.

▶ *You can buy plant ties at your local garden centre, or use food bag ties or string.*

Pinch out

On tall varieties, pinch out (or take off) the main stem that starts to grow above the fourth truss, or cluster of flowers. If the plant is left to grow tall, any fruit would struggle to **ripen**.

SCIENCE SPOT *Leaves*
Don't pull off all the leaves (right). It is the leaves that work hard to turn sunlight, water and **carbon dioxide** into a store of energy to help the plant grow. This process is called photosynthesis.

▲ *Removing side-shoots also helps the plants concentrate on growing fruit.*

Problem page!

A lot of problems with growing tomatoes come from watering — either too much or too little. If you tend them well and every day, then you may avoid many of the problems.

▲ Tomato plants do not like their leaves to be wet all the time. If the weather is bad, try to cover them in some way.

Water carefully!

Irregular watering — not watering for a long time and then watering a lot — can lead to **blossom end rot** (see opposite) or cause the tomatoes to swell and split. Under-watering may make your plant lose its flowers and fruit. Over-watering can make fruit lose flavour.

▶ You can tell a lot about the health of the plant by looking at its leaves — if they look healthy, your plant will be healthy, too.

◄ This plant's leaves show that it is unwell. It may have been over-watered.

◄ This tomato has split because the soil dried out and then too much water was given at once, making the fruit swell too quickly.

Blossom end rot

Blossom end rot turns the end of the tomato (where the blossom was) brown. It can be caused by irregular watering and allowing your plants to dry out.

Tomato blight

Tomatoes, like potatoes, can get **blight**. This is a disease that turns the leaves and fruit brown. It is more common in very wet weather.

◄ If your tomatoes get blight, it is best to get rid of any infected plants and fruit.

Getting ready for harvest

It won't be long now until all your hard work will pay off.

Green tomatoes

Your plants probably already have some bright yellow flowers. You will soon notice small, green tomatoes begin to develop in place of your flowers. In a few weeks, they will grow and ripen in the sun.

▲ Once you have flowers, keep an eye out for the first tomato fruits.

◀ ▼ It's very exciting when you see your first fruits.

SCIENCE SPOT *Pollination*

Pollination is a process where **pollen** from the flower of one plant is transferred to another plant of the same type. This allows the plant to grow fruits and seeds to make new plants. Tomato plants are self-fertilising, meaning that they can grow fruit without needing pollen to be taken from one plant to another by a visiting insect.

Feed your plants

You will need to feed any plants in pots or grow-bags with tomato fertiliser. Ask your grown-up helper to do this with you. Be sure to follow instructions, but start when the first small fruits have appeared.

Red and ripe

When the tomatoes are red (if they are a red variety!), they are ripe and ready to pick. To get your tomatoes at their best and with the most flavour, pick them as soon as they turn red.

▲ *You can buy tomato fertiliser from a garden centre.*

◀ *Tomatoes are ready to harvest when they come away from the stalk easily when you pull gently.*

▶ *Those tiny seeds you planted 20 weeks ago are now ripe tomatoes in your hands. Enjoy!*

Tasty tomatoes

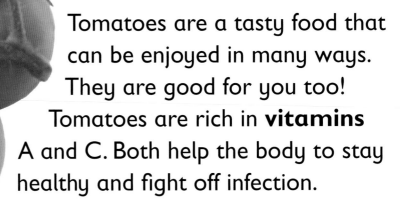

Tomatoes are a tasty food that can be enjoyed in many ways. They are good for you too! Tomatoes are rich in **vitamins** A and C. Both help the body to stay healthy and fight off infection.

Preparing your tomatoes

Before you get creative with your tomatoes, you need to give them a good wash in cold water. If you're not going to eat them straight away it's best to store them in the fridge, but tomatoes are best eaten at room temperature for flavour.

Many uses

Can you imagine chips without tomato ketchup or a BLT (bacon, lettuce and tomato) sandwich without the 'T'? Tomatoes are used in many recipes. Why not try the recipe opposite, or search the Internet for more ideas.

◀ *Tomatoes can be part of a quick snack, a sauce or a main meal.*

Tomato sauce

Ingredients

- 1 kg tomatoes, chopped
- 1 small onion, sliced
- 25 grams brown sugar
- 1 cup vinegar (or cider vinegar)
- 1 teaspoon (tsp) allspice
- 1 tsp salt
- 1 tablespoon (tbsp) paprika
- 1 tsp white pepper

Method

Ask an adult to help you with the chopping and cooking parts.

1. With your adult helper, simmer the tomatoes and onions until soft.

2. Press the mixture through a sieve, then place it back into the pan and add the sugar, vinegar, spices, and so on.

3. Let it bubble until the mixture is quite thick. Remember to keep stirring to stop the sauce sticking to the bottom of the pan, especially once it starts to get thicker!

4. Pour the sauce into **sterilised** bottles and put the top on.

This should make around 500 ml of sauce.

▶ *You could eat your tomato sauce with chips or put it on a pizza base!*

27

Gardening calendar

Here's an 'at-a-glance' guide to the growing year. Planting and growing times vary, depending on where you live, but you can follow these general guidelines.

Sow or plant	Tend / Prepare	Harvest
	Late winter (Jan–Feb) Plan your crop; choose your tomato varieties.	
Sow seeds in pots on windowsill indoors in the middle of this period.	**Early spring** (March–April) Check and water seedlings regularly.	
Begin to harden off seedlings.	**Late spring** (April–May) Water, weed and feed plants. Stake any tall, cordon varieties.	
Plant seedlings out at beginning of this period.	**Early summer** (June–July) Water, weed and feed plants.	First tomatoes will be ready for harvesting at the end of this period.
	Late summer (July–Aug)	Plants will continue to fruit throughout this period.
	Early autumn (Sept–Oct)	Plants will fruit through to mid to late autumn.
	Late autumn (Oct–Nov) Dig plot over, digging in compost or manure.	

Gardening glossary

blight: a disease that affects plants, making the produce rot.

blossom end rot: a disease that turns one end of a tomato (the flower end) brown.

carbon dioxide: a gas that is part of the air around us.

compost: a mixture of soil and rotted plants used to fertilise, or feed, plants to help them grow.

conditions: the situation or surroundings that affect something.

diseases: illnesses that can be caught by plants and animals.

fertiliser: a substance such as manure or a chemical mixture used to make soil more fertile (better for growing plants).

germinate: the point when a root and leaf break through a seed case and the seed begins to grow.

grow-bag: a specially made plastic bag of soil and compost for growing plants in.

hardy: able to survive under poor or extreme weather.

plant on: when you move seedlings or plants from one growing place to another in order to give them more space to grow.

pollen: the powder from a flower that is needed to complete the fertilisation process.

ripen: when a fruit is fully formed and ready to be picked.

root: the part of a plant below the ground that takes water and nutrients, or goodness, from the soil to the rest of the plant.

seed: a tiny thing that a plant can grow from.

seedling: the young plant grown from a seed.

sheltered: in this case, a spot that is out of the wind.

shoot: new growth from a plant or seed.

sterilised: glass bottles can be sterilised (made free from bacteria) by putting them in very hot water, followed by the oven. This should be done by an adult.

truss: a group, or cluster, of flowers.

varieties: different types of the same plant family.

vitamin: natural substances in food that are good for your body and health.

Index

Useful websites

www.bbc.co.uk/gardening/ gardening_with_children/

www.gardeningwithchildren.co.uk
Gardening activities and information about how plants grow.

www.rhs.org.uk/schoolgardening
Find out about school gardening projects and clubs or play the gardening game.

www.bbc.co.uk/digin/tomato.shtml
Fun, animated clip on how to grow tomatoes from seed.

Gardening club

Have you enjoyed growing your own? How about joining a gardening club? Your school may have one. You could grow fruit and vegetables which could be cooked and eaten as part of your school meals and snacks, or make ladybird homes to help attract them to your garden. If your school doesn't have a gardening club, why not talk to your teacher about setting one up?

Note to parents and teachers: Every effort has been made by the Publishers to ensure that these websites are suitable for children, that they are of the highest educational value, and that they contain no inappropriate or offensive material. However, because of the nature of the Internet, it is impossible to guarantee that the contents of these sites will not be altered. We strongly advise that Internet access is supervised by a responsible adult.